230 million years ago, all land is united as the supercontinent of Pangaea. The Mesozoic Era, or "Age of Dinosaurs," begins—an era of super-oceans and super monsters. The earth will be terrorized for more than 160 million years. Then, 63 million years ago, the Mesozoic will end. Pangaea will split into a northern (Laurasia) and southern (Gondwanaland) continent, later fragmenting into the continents we know today. The Mesozoic is divided into three periods, the most ancient being the Triassic Period (230 to 180 million years ago), then the Jurassic (180 to 135 million years ago), and the Cretaceous Period (135 to 63 million years ago).

During the Early Triassic, much of Pangaea, especially its northern regions, is deserts and steppes with scattered salt lakes. Some conifers exist (Voltzia), but vegetation is sparse. Podopteryx and Longisquama are bizarre denizens of this inhospitable world. Only recently unearthed, these Soviet oddities incite lively arguments among scientists.

Feather-like structures appear to issue from the back of hummingbird-sized Longisquama. A Russian paleontologist believes these false-feathers were used as a parachute to break the creature's leaping falls. One scientist believes they could be used as threat devices; another suggests they extruded from the anterior limbs, rather than along the back.

On a stone slab containing the mouse-sized skeleton of Podopteryx are skin impressions. These show leather-like flaps of skin stretched between the front and back legs, and also the hind legs and tail. Podopteryx must have resembled a "flying squirrel" as it glided from tree to tree.

These delicate animals are so unusual that new families have been created to accommodate them (Longisquamidae and Podopterygidae). They probably belong to the larger order Thecodontia, although this has not been absolutely proven.

Podopteryx

Equisetites

Schizoneura

Pleuromeia

Longisquama

(The flora illustrated is based on Early Triassic specimens from Russia and Germany.)

There is much variation among thecodonts, so it is difficult to generalize about them. They are usually large-headed, sharp-toothed predators. The neck is never very long or slender, and the body is nearly always provided with some sort of armor. The hind legs are always considerably longer than the fore ones, and in some thecodonts, there is a tendency toward bipedalism (walking only on the back legs).

Thecodonts undoubtedly include the ancestors of crocodiles, and perhaps are also the precursors of pterosaurs, dinosaurs, and ultimately birds by way of dinosaurs.

With the exception of birds, all of these groups are included in the Archosauria, traditionally considered a subclass of reptiles. However, fascinating recent studies by Prof. John H. Ostrom (Yale), Dr. Robert T. Bakker (Harvard), and Dr. Armand Riqles (University of Paris) firmly point to endothermy ("warm-bloodedness") in most archosaurs. These studies have led Dr. Bakker to up-grade the archosaurs to the status of a full Class, distinct from the ectothermic ("cold-blooded") reptiles.* Birds are grouped under this new class by Bakker.

A series of Middle Triassic thecodonts has recently been discovered in the Chanares Formation of La Rioja Provence, north-western Argentina. Investigations of Chanares deposition suggest that more than two hundred fifteen million years ago, this portion of Argentina was provided with some lakes, around which animal communities flourished.

Four-foot-long *Chanaresuchus*, a big-headed, feebly armored thecodont, seems well-adapted to live an amphibious, croco-dile-like existence in Chanares lakes. It belongs to the family Proterochamp- sidae, known also in southern Brazil and perhaps in Tanzania, East Africa. The proterochampsids continue to the dawn of late Triassic times.

Lightly constructed *Gracilisuchus* is a quick-moving, possibly semi-bipedal thecodont. Unlike its more primitive neighbor *Chanaresuchus*, it prefers a dry ter-rain on which to pursue its preda-ceous activities.

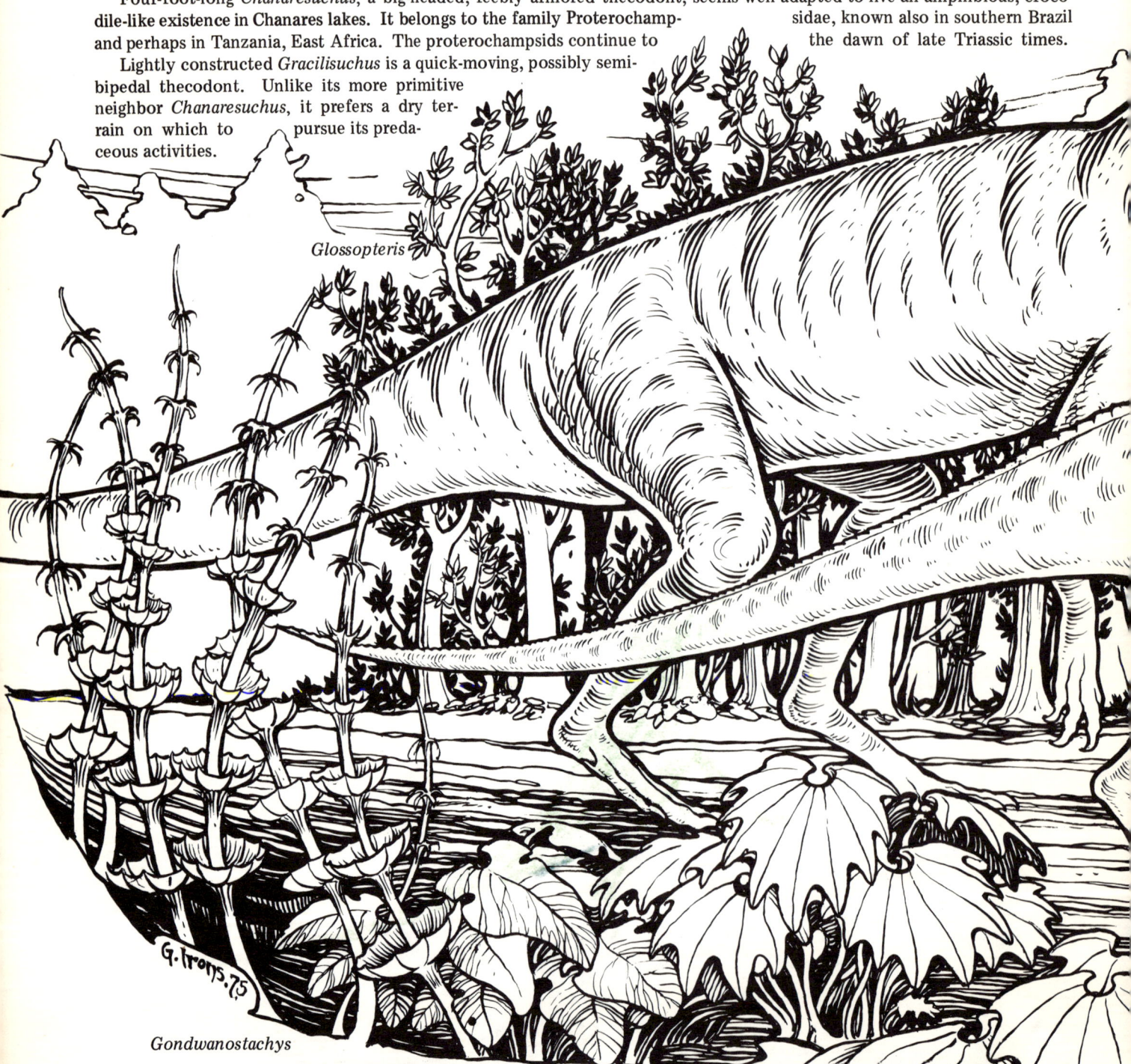

Glossopteris

G. Irons. 75

Gondwanostachys

(No plants have been collected from the Chanares, so we have used specimens from roughly contemporary Argentine formations for our landscape.)

Hausmannia

Note: In these illustrations we have tried to include plants contemporary with the animals represented, using frora from or near the regions where the fossil animals were found.

*Although the evidence so far accumulated seems to be in favor of endothermy (vs. ectothermy) in dinosaurs, much more work needs to be done before this view can be fully accepted; the elevation of Archosauria to full class status seems premature at present.

Chanaresuchus

Baierophyllites

Gracilisuchus

Chiropteris

Barrealia

Voltzia

Otozamites

Pelourdea

While *Chanaresuchus* thrives in Argentina, the waters of the ancestral Mediterranean Sea (called the Tethys) extend eastward from Spain as far as China. The modern Black and Caspian Seas are mere remnants of this ancient expanse. On a northern shore of the Tethys (now Monte San Giorgio, Switzerland) live a variety of extremely primitive lizards and lizard relatives.

Lizards differ from their ancestors, the eosuchians, in a variety of features, but the most important distinction is exhibited on the side of the skull behind the orbits. In eosuchians, lizards, and archosaurs, two openings lie just in back of the eyes, one above the other. Lizards, however, differ from eosuchians and archosaurs in lacking a bar of bone below the lower opening. This allows considerable bone movement along the posterior corner of the skull.

Peculiar *Tanystropheus* qualifies for lizard-hood through skull structure and other essential details, but nevertheless, it certainly does not bear much semblance to modern forms. Its giraffe-like neck appears to have been designed by a plumber from pipes. Dr. Rupert Wild (University of Zürich) has recently conducted investigations on twenty-five more or less complete skeletons of *Tanystropheus*. He demonstrates a series of growth stages from young individuals under two feet long, to old fellows nearly twenty feet in length. The back teeth of especially immature creatures are three-pronged, but larger specimens possess sharp, conical teeth throughout. Dr. Wild believes these differences indicate radically contrasting diets, the little fellows devouring insects on Tethyan shores, the larger ones (probably outfitted with hind paddles) living a marine existence on squid and fish.

Fragmentary evidence of an extremely large *Tanystropheus* was recently discovered in Wadi Ramon, Israel. This individual must have been thirty to forty feet in length.

Paul Olsen (Yale University) has recently discovered a series of small reptiles from the Late Triassic of eastern North America. In this menagerie of little fellows, Olsen reports a long-necked creature which may prove to be a tanystrophid relative. Unlike *Tanystropheus* it has a tail provided with two pairs of sharp spikes.

Neuropteridium

Tanystropheus

Pterophyllum

Anomopteris

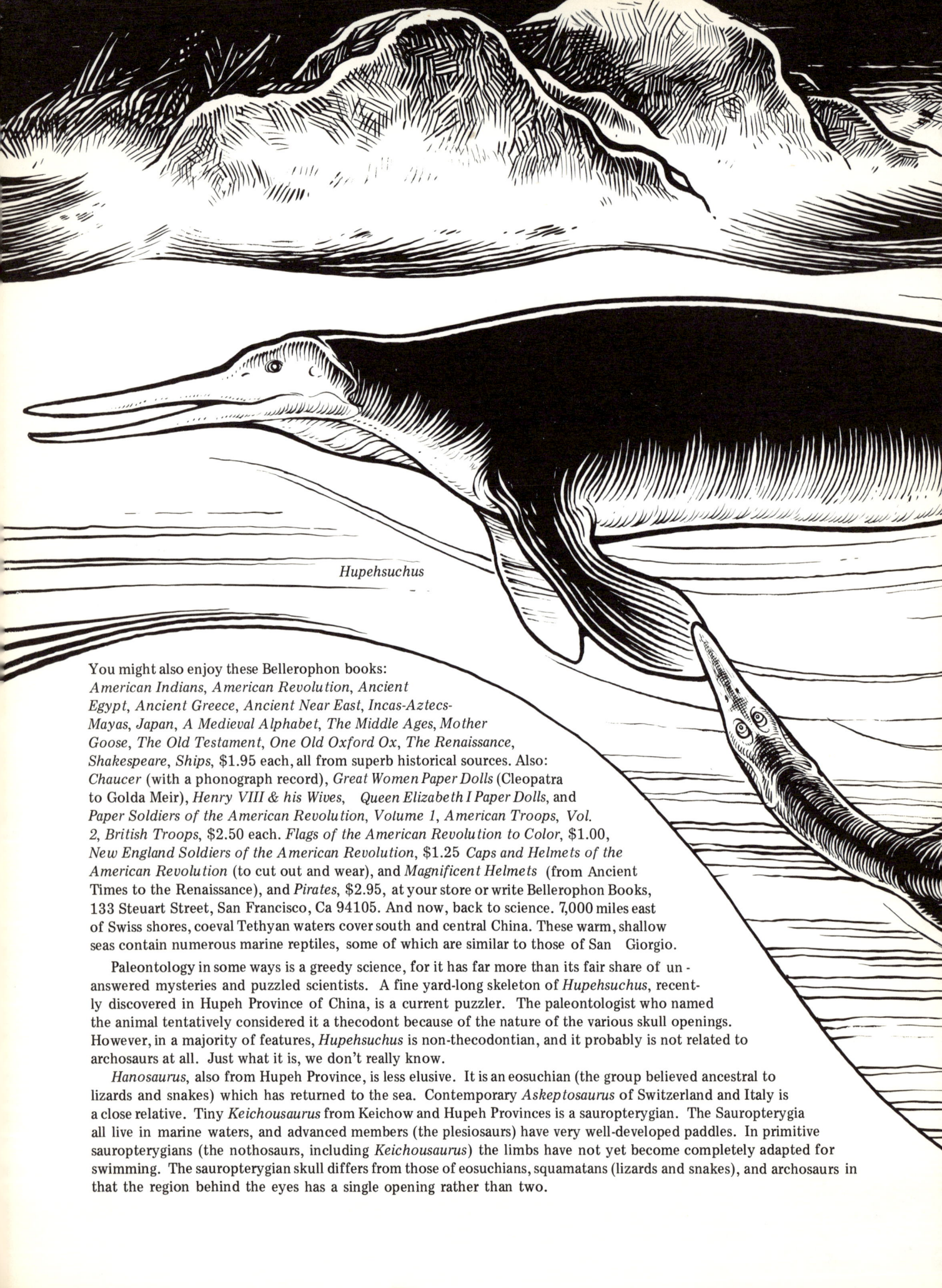

Hupehsuchus

You might also enjoy these Bellerophon books:
American Indians, American Revolution, Ancient Egypt, Ancient Greece, Ancient Near East, Incas-Aztecs-Mayas, Japan, A Medieval Alphabet, The Middle Ages, Mother Goose, The Old Testament, One Old Oxford Ox, The Renaissance, Shakespeare, Ships, $1.95 each, all from superb historical sources. Also: *Chaucer* (with a phonograph record), *Great Women Paper Dolls* (Cleopatra to Golda Meir), *Henry VIII & his Wives, Queen Elizabeth I Paper Dolls,* and *Paper Soldiers of the American Revolution, Volume 1, American Troops, Vol. 2, British Troops,* $2.50 each. *Flags of the American Revolution to Color,* $1.00, *New England Soldiers of the American Revolution,* $1.25 *Caps and Helmets of the American Revolution* (to cut out and wear), and *Magnificent Helmets* (from Ancient Times to the Renaissance), and *Pirates,* $2.95, at your store or write Bellerophon Books, 133 Steuart Street, San Francisco, Ca 94105. And now, back to science. 7,000 miles east of Swiss shores, coeval Tethyan waters cover south and central China. These warm, shallow seas contain numerous marine reptiles, some of which are similar to those of San Giorgio.

Paleontology in some ways is a greedy science, for it has far more than its fair share of un-answered mysteries and puzzled scientists. A fine yard-long skeleton of *Hupehsuchus*, recently discovered in Hupeh Province of China, is a current puzzler. The paleontologist who named the animal tentatively considered it a thecodont because of the nature of the various skull openings. However, in a majority of features, *Hupehsuchus* is non-thecodontian, and it probably is not related to archosaurs at all. Just what it is, we don't really know.

Hanosaurus, also from Hupeh Province, is less elusive. It is an eosuchian (the group believed ancestral to lizards and snakes) which has returned to the sea. Contemporary *Askeptosaurus* of Switzerland and Italy is a close relative. Tiny *Keichousaurus* from Keichow and Hupeh Provinces is a sauropterygian. The Sauropterygia all live in marine waters, and advanced members (the plesiosaurs) have very well-developed paddles. In primitive sauropterygians (the nothosaurs, including *Keichousaurus*) the limbs have not yet become completely adapted for swimming. The sauropterygian skull differs from those of eosuchians, squamatans (lizards and snakes), and archosaurs in that the region behind the eyes has a single opening rather than two.

Hanosaurus

Keichousaurus

G. Irons · 75

Pelourdea

The famous Petrified Forest of northeastern Arizona dates back to Late Triassic times, 200 million years ago. During the early deposition of the Chinle Formation, giant trees *(Araucarioxylon)*, possibly relatives of contemporary southern araucarian trees, abound. So dense are these stands of trees that branches issue forth only near the tree tops, as much as 200 feet above ground. Few creatures come here. Beyond the forests, in ponds and swamps, animal life frolics. A large pond, near what is now St. Johns, Arizona, attracts numerous animals. Nearly 40 rhinocerous-sized therapsids (extinct rela tives of mammals) live here. These herbivores *(Placerias)* are from a heavily-built line called dicyno-donts. The toothless jaws of *Placerias* were doubtless equipped with a horny sheath, like a bird's beak. Males have upper tusks near the front of the mouth for uprooting large plants.

A few Aetosaurs, herbivorous, armadillo-like thecodonts, are here. *Desmatosuchus*, with curved shoulder spikes, is a large aetosaur, sometimes more than fifteen feet long.

This region is not without its predators. Phytosaurs (aquatic, crocodile-like thecodonts) live here permanently. Most of them are fairly small (6 - 10 feet) members of the narrow-snouted genus, *Rutiodon*. Other specimens of *Rutiodon* nearby are 20 or 30 feet long, and the later broad-snouted Chinle phytosaur *Nicrosaurus* is even larger than that.

The chief terror here is an unnamed creature of the thecodont family Rauisuchidae. This 12-foot quadruped, unlike phytosaurs, is an active, land-dwelling predator with a deep skull, many sharp teeth, and a row of small, bony plates lining its back. It may possibly hunt the giant *Placerias* in packs, like wolves.

Pelourde

All plants in the Chinle scene based on Chinle specimens.

Desmatosuchus

Nilssoniopter

unnamed aetosaurid

Clathropteris

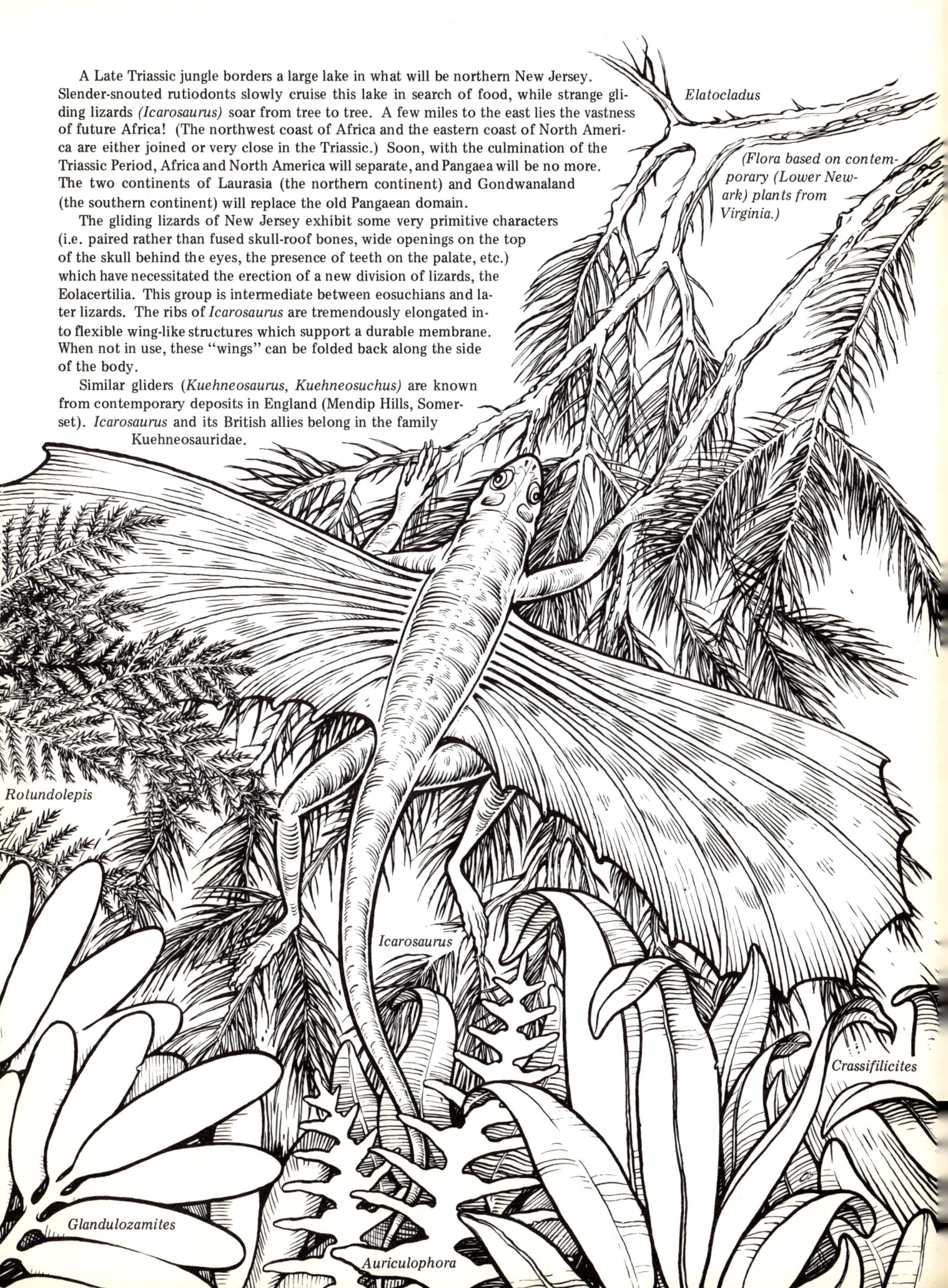

A Late Triassic jungle borders a large lake in what will be northern New Jersey. Slender-snouted rutiodonts slowly cruise this lake in search of food, while strange gliding lizards *(Icarosaurus)* soar from tree to tree. A few miles to the east lies the vastness of future Africa! (The northwest coast of Africa and the eastern coast of North America are either joined or very close in the Triassic.) Soon, with the culmination of the Triassic Period, Africa and North America will separate, and Pangaea will be no more. The two continents of Laurasia (the northern continent) and Gondwanaland (the southern continent) will replace the old Pangaean domain.

The gliding lizards of New Jersey exhibit some very primitive characters (i.e. paired rather than fused skull-roof bones, wide openings on the top of the skull behind the eyes, the presence of teeth on the palate, etc.) which have necessitated the erection of a new division of lizards, the Eolacertilia. This group is intermediate between eosuchians and later lizards. The ribs of *Icarosaurus* are tremendously elongated into flexible wing-like structures which support a durable membrane. When not in use, these "wings" can be folded back along the side of the body.

Similar gliders *(Kuehneosaurus, Kuehneosuchus)* are known from contemporary deposits in England (Mendip Hills, Somerset). *Icarosaurus* and its British allies belong in the family Kuehneosauridae.

Elatocladus

(Flora based on contemporary (Lower Newark) plants from Virginia.)

Rotundolepis

Icarosaurus

Crassifilicites

Glandulozamites

Auriculophora

In the Late Triassic,* northwestern Argentina is a land of thick jungles, swamps, and lakes. Torrential rains frequently occur, and the climate is humid and hot. Animals abound. The Los Colorados Formation is undergoing deposition. Largely through the efforts of one man, Dr. Jose Bonaparte of the University of Tucuman, the ancient wonders of the Los Colorados currently are revealing themselves to the scientific world.

Thecodonts are especially numerous in these pre-Andean jungles. All are rather small, with few, if any, exceeding the hundred pound mark. *Riojasuchus* is the most dangerous of the Los Colorados thecodonts. Its short, mordacious jaws bear few teeth, but those present are extremely large and dagger-like. *Riojasuchus* belongs in the Ornithosuchidae, a Middle and Late Triassic family best represented in the southern regions.

Dr. Alick D. Walker (University of Newcastle-upon-Tyne) believes the ornithosuchids are primitive dinosaurs. We, however, follow Dr. Bonaparte and others, and envision the ornithosuchids as a sterile line of thecodonts.

Greyhound-proportioned *Pseudhesperosuchus* is one of the most agile of thecodonts. In several features, such as its elongated wrist elements and the structure of the shoulder girdle, *Pseudhesperosuchus* is very crocodile-like. Scientists are currently divided in regarding this creature and its allies (the Sphenosuchidae) as crocodile-like thecodonts, or thecodont-like crocodiles. We presently favor a thecodont relationship.

*In the Late Triassic, a new product, the mammal, first appears in tiny mouse-sized packaging.

(No plants have been identified from the Los Colorados Formation, though some fern fronds and wood have been collected in these sediments; therefore, we have used roughly contemporary plants from other Argentine formations for our illustrations.)

Linguifolium

Cardiopteridium

Ctenis

Thaumatopteris

Dicroidium

Baiera

Riojasuchus

Ginkgodium

Pseudhesperosuchus

Cardiopteridium

Dinosaurs represent two orders (Saurischia, Ornithischia) of scaled*, egg-laying animals which assume an erect, rather than sprawling posture. They are probably warm-blooded and many are capable of rapid movement. Dinosaurs differ from thecodonts primarily in their perfection of an erect posture and a greater tendency towards gigantism.

The saurischians (so-called "lizard-hipped" dinosaurs) differ from the ornithischians ("bird-hipped" dinosaurs) in a number of rather technical characters. A primary difference, as you might guess, is seen in the pelvis. In the Saurischia, the two lower pelvic bones (pubis and ischium) converge at right angles to one another when they contact the upper pelvic bone, the ilium. In ornithischians, the two

Aslerotheca

Dicroidium

Dicroidium

Yabeiella

Cladophlebis

lower bones run parallel to each other. Few saurischians develop any kind of armor; Ornithischians usually have plenty of armor. Many saurischians eat meat; in contrast, all ornithischians are plant-eaters.

The most majestic of Los Colorados swamp-dwellers is the 20-foot dinosaur, *Riojasaurus*. This early saurischian belongs to the suborder Sauropodomorpha, a group of small-headed, lengthy-necked herbivores which sometimes attain colossal proportions. The famous brontosaurs (properly known as sauropods) are giant sauropodomorphs successful in the later Mesozoic.

Riojasaurus is a prosauropod, a group of primitive sauropodomorphs abundant in the late Triassic times, then tapering off completely during the early phases of the Jurassic Period. Numerous paleontologists have attempted to segregate prosauropods into families, but never with complete success. Lightly built to moderately heavy forms with rather small front limbs (semi-bipeds?) are currently included in one family, the Anchisauridae. Especially massive creatures with particularly big forelimbs (undoubtedly quadrupeds) are placed in the Melanorosauridae (including *Riojasaurus*).

Early Jurassic *Vulcanodon* from Rhodesia, the last and largest melanorosaur, may have been as much as 40 feet, probably outweighing an elephant. Four-toed footprints of early melanorosaurs *(Pseudotetrasauropus)* have been reported from the Lower Stormberg Series of Lesotho, in southern Africa, and from d'Anduze, France. Very large, five-toed footprints *(Pentasauropus, Tetrasauropus)*, representing an unknown prosauropod family, were discovered at Lesotho with the melanorosaur tracks.

*Recent evidence (discussed later) suggests that some small dinosaurs may have had feathers.

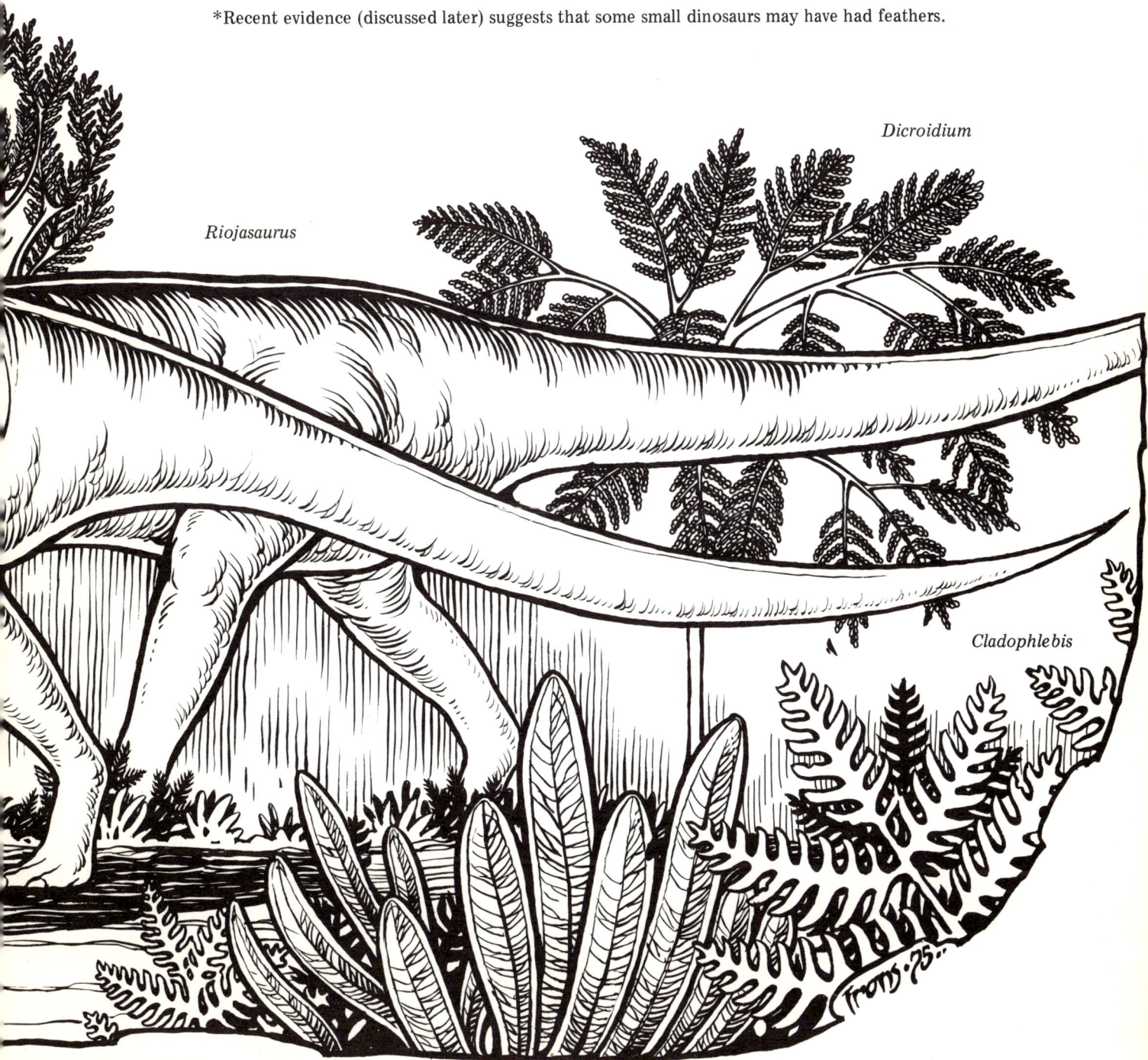

Dicroidium

Riojasaurus

Cladophlebis

Yabeiella

During the final stages of the Triassic or the dawn of the Jurassic (between 200 to 175 million years ago), as the Kayenta Formation is being deposited, northeastern Arizona and southern Utah is a land of floodplains, lakes, and ponds. Small, blunt-toothed sharks (*Acrodus*) and thick-scaled fish *(Semionotus)* inhabit these freshwater bodies.

The floodplains coat hundreds of square miles of terrain with a sticky, damp mud, and countless numbers of dinosaurs, all three-toed and bipedal, ornament the earth with their bird-like footprints. (Centuries ago, near what is now Kanab, Utah, members of a long-lost Indian tribe carved petroglyphs depicting the footprints on a cliff-face.)

In drier areas, near rocks and under clumps and vegetation, weasel-sized, plant-eating tritylodonts (advanced mammal-like creatures) live a secretive existence. Short-faced, pigmy crocodiles, less than half a yard in length, are also present.

Twenty-foot, double-crested *Dilophosaurus* undoubtedly is responsible for many of the three-toed footprints. It belongs to the theropod division of the Saurischia. Theropods are the most bird-like of all dinosaurs, and there is little doubt this suborder gave rise to the birds. All theropods are bipedal* with generally reduced front limbs, and the vast majority are carnivorous, so sharp teeth and claws are typical. The long hind legs are especially powerful and built for high speed; these terminate in very bird-like feet. Unlike most other theropods, *Dilophosaurus* has a very delicately constructed skull, suggesting it killed its prey with its great taloned hind feet, rather than by using its weak jaws. A similar hunting technique was probably used by another, larger-crested Kayentan dinosaur currently being studied.

Araucarites

Clathropteris

Dictyophyllum

* Supposed quadrupedal theropod footprints have been described from Argentina; however, their true affinities have not been proven. (The flora of the Kayenta Formation is unknown; our restoration is based on contemporary plants with world-wide distribution.)

Clathropteris

Dilophosaurus

Near the close of the Triassic period, the upper Stormberg Series is being deposited in South Africa, then a vast desertland wedged between Argentina and Antarctica.* An occasional oasis, inhabited by plants and animals, breaks the barren desert monotony. The fossil record indicates these fertile areas by remains of large tree trunks belonging to giant seed-ferns, *Rhexoxylon*.

A few partial ... skeletons of several animals have been discovered in upper Stormberg rocks. The most fre- quent crea- ... ture is the prosauropod dinosaur *Massospondylus*. *Massospondylus* differs from melan- orosaurs in ... a generally smaller, lighter build. This allies it with the cosmopolitan family Anchisau- ridae. *Mas-* ... *sospondylus* jaws are lined with both powerful, serrated teeth and weak teeth for plants. Per- ... haps the dinosaur varies his diet, or maybe the sharp teeth are his protection.

Recently several types of ornithischian dinosaurs have been discovered in the upper Stormberg Beds. The families of Fabrosauridae and Heterodontosauridae are represented. The yard-long herbivorous fabrosaurs are, like heterodontosaurs, strictly bipedal, light-boned dinosaurs. They differ from heterodontosaurs primarily in dental makeup. In fabrosaurs, the tooth row is continuous with the outer jaw margin rather than recessed inward, as in the heterodontosaurs. The great majority of ornithischians have recessed tooth rows similar to those found in mammals. It has been suggested that these ornithischians possessed muscular cheeks just as mammals do. The fabrosaurs, in contrast, were cheekless, like reptiles today. The Fabrosauridae are equipped only with leaf-shaped teeth, while the Heterodontosauridae have knife-like teeth as well.

Fabrosaur-like dinosaurs are also known from the late Triassic of Morocco (*Azendohsaurus*) and the Late Jurassic of England (*Echinodon*).

Dicroidium

Massospondylus

* By the end of the Triassic, Antarctica will have separated from Africa.

Sphenobaiera

The flora illustrated is based on Lower Stormberg (Molteno) specimens, because only wood comes from the upper Stormberg. We have no guarantee that plants other than Dicroidium *exist at this time in South Africa.*

Rissikia

fabrosaur, new genus

Taeniopteris

Rienitzia

Irons 75

Kurtzia

Doratophyllum

Ptilozamites

Bjuvia

Drepanozamites

Gerrothorax

Neocalamites

As deserts envelope South Africa, seas push across much of Europe. The remaining arid or semi-arid climate is replaced by a cooler, humid one. Swamps and lagoons are common. The lower levels of the Höganäs Series, a coal-bearing formation in Scania, Sweden, yield, through fossil impressions, a detailed picture of latest Triassic plant life. Some animal remains such as *Gerrothorax* come from this series.

On the dark bottom of a deep, brackish Scanian lagoon, an awesome creature, *Gerrothorax*, lies motionless, practically hidden in the cold mud. Its enormous, dorsally-directed eyes spot a thick-scaled fish nearby, and instantly seal-like hind flippers and tail propel it to its target.

As do many modern amphibians, *Gerrothorax* retains its gills throughout life, rather than losing them with adulthood. Its flat body is armored on top and bottom. *Gerrothorax* and its broad-headed relatives belong in the Plagiosauridae, a family of labyrinthodonts living throughout Europe during middle and Late Triassic times. Labyrinthodonts are an ancient subclass of primitive amphibians especially common in Paleozoic times; *Gerrothorax* is perhaps the last member of this group. (The plants illustrated all come from the lower Höganäs Series (*Lepidopteris ottonis* Zone) of Scania.)

G. Irons '75

England, one hundred and eighty million years ago, is almost entirely blanketed with muddy seas. A large island (Brabant Island) provides smooth, sandy beaches in what will be southeastern England in the future. To the north, where Scotland will later exist, a series of islands, or perhaps a single, low body of land, houses jungles and great, land-dwelling creatures. To the west, the eastern shores of a great land mass (North Atlantis) majestically rise above the waters.

The dawn of the Jurassic Period is here and Lower Lias sediments are being deposited. As in the latest Triassic times, Europe continues its submission to shallow seas dotted with islands and archipelagos. Though muddy, the English seas generally swarm with curious reptiles and fishes.

The largest and most dangerous of the sea monsters in these waters is *Temnodontosaurus*, an ichthyosaur. The ichthyosaurs are true reptiles which develop many fishlike features because of their ocean-dwelling habits. The limbs become paddles, the tail is equipped with a large fin, and the body becomes streamlined and torpedo-like. These modifications allow ichthyosaurs to dart through the muddy depths at great speeds while in pursuit of food, which consists of fish and smaller reptiles. Most of these reptiles are less than ten feet in length, but *Temnodontosaurus* grows to nearly thirty feet. An unnamed ichthyosaur from the Late Triassic (Lunning Formation) of central Nevada was much larger. Ichthyosaurs are so different from other reptiles that they have been placed in a subclass (Ichthyopterygia) of their own. They have no descendants and we know nothing about their ancestors.

Eight-foot long *Plesiosaurus*, looking very much like a great sea-serpent of fishermen's lore, represents another group of fish-eating, marine reptiles (Sauropterygia), mentioned earlier.

Chondrosteus

Temnodontosaurus

Metopacanthus

Plesiosaurus

Squaloraja

Palaeospinax

Eomesodon

Irons·75

Very infrequently the carcass of a land-dweller will drift out to sea and be buried in the Lower Lias mud. Along the Dorset coast of southern England (Lyme Regis, Charmouth), and in central England (Warwick, Leicester) nineteenth and twentieth century collectors were fortunate enough to find isolated bones, partial, and sometimes even nearly complete skeletons of these terrestrial creatures. Remains of armored ornithischians (scelidosaurs), medium-sized theropods (sarcosaurs), giant theropods (genera indeterminate), and ancient fliers (dimorphodonts) have thus far been recovered. The Mendip Hills of west England yield another rare vision of earliest Jurassic land life. Here weasel-sized tritylodonts *(Oligokyphus)* lived in considerable numbers in the rocky highlands well above the shoreline. Instead of being deposited in the watery depths of the sea, their bones are preserved at or near their actual dwelling places.*

Dimorphodon looks more like a demon created from the chimeric visions of Hieronymus Bosch than a real flesh and blood animal. It is a pterosaur, but just what are pterosaurs is a question currently plaguing some scientists. Traditionally these grotesque oddities have been called "flying reptiles." However, hair-like structures were noted on an extremely well-preserved German specimen *(Rhamphorhynchus)* some years ago, and the recent discovery of a new "hair"-covered Russian pterosaur *(Sordes)* suggests all pterosaurians were probably insulated with such a covering. This

Pagiophyllum

Scelidosaurus

Williamsoniella

Clathropterus

Oligokyphus

* The Mendip Hills also provide an important fauna of Late Triassic land vertebrates including early mammals, icarosaur-like lizards, rhynchocephalians, tiny crocodiles, and a small dinosaur.

plus other more elaborate data strongly indicates these creatures were warm-blooded just as mammals and birds are today, and are possibly not closely related to the cold-blooded, non-insulated reptiles. Pterosaurs apparently evolved from a thecodont ancestor in Triassic times, and are probably archosaurians. However, a South African paleontologist, Dr. A. S. Brink, considers pterosaurs in a class of their own.

The two Pterosaurian suborders are the primitive Rhamphorhynchoidea (including *Dimorphodon*) and the more advanced Pterodactyloidea. The deep rhamphorhynchoid skull, armed with rows of teeth, is not long, and there are two openings on the face in front of the eye sockets. The neck and metacarpal bones are short. The hind foot usually has five well-developed toes, and the tail is very long. Pterodactyloids are long and low-headed with a single opening near the eyes. Their slender teeth, usually reduced to the front of the jaws, are sometimes absent. Characteristic of these forms are long necks and metacarpals; the fifth toe of the hind foot is greatly reduced, and the pterodactyloid tail is always quite short.

Dimorphodon

(Flora based on English Lower Lias specimens and contemporary plants from other European regions.)

Paracycas

Dimorphodon

Clathropteris

Sciadopitys
(umbrella pine)

Sciadopitys
(umbrella pine)

Elatides

Dacentrurus

Matonidium

Irons.75.

During pre-Jurassic times the Ornithischia certainly
did not do their share in furnishing the animal world with fantastic creations. Late
Triassic ornithischians occur in South and North Africa, Europe, East Asia, Nova Sco-
tia, and South America, apparently yet only as small, lightly built bipeds, all belonging to the suborder Ornithopoda.
Shame! With the Jurassic, as if to make up for lost time, the ornithischians radiate in some fascinating directions. Small
ornithopods continue, but now large, stocky ornithopods (iguanodonts) accompany them.* Island-dwelling, well-armored scelidosaurs appear very early in the Jurassic. Nature introduces, surely with a chuckle, still another new ornithischian product
to the Jurassic world—the amazing stegosaur. What P. T. Barnum would have given for a stegosaur!

The earliest stegosaur remains are meager (160 million years old)- a few broken bones and armor plates from the Inferior
Oolite series (early Middle Jurassic) of England. With Late Jurassic times, the stegosaurian suborder diversifies into several distinctive genera differing primarily in type of armature, limb proportions, and pelvic features. (Our illustrations demonstrate
stegosaur form amply, so we need not describe it here.)

Fifteen-foot-long *Dacentrurus*, present in Kimmeridgian rocks of southern England and elsewhere, differs from other stegosaurs in altogether lacking armor plates (so pleasingly exhibited in the American *Stegosaurus*). Instead, only massive spikes line
the back and tail. Relatively long front limbs and short neural spines also characterize this animal.

*The authors recently identified some large, iguanodont-like trackways in early Jurassic sediments in Utah.

Ginkgo

Ginkgo

Todites

Hausmannia

Dacentrurus

Todites

The great African continent is beginning its separation from South America by Late Jurassic times. A rift has already sliced northward from South Africa to Nigeria and the former has probably already broken contact with South America, resulting in the birth of the Southern Atlantic Ocean.

On the opposite side of Africa, in what is now Tendaguru in Tanzania, numerous dinosaurs are living out their lives in total ignorance of the current fragmentation of their world. The sediments at Tendaguru accumulate in a large, slow river one hundred and forty-five million years ago. The sea is nearby, perhaps separated by a sand bar. Twice the sea penetrates this barrier, forcing the dinosaur population to migrate to other drier regions.

The forty-foot long Tendaguru dinosaur *Dicraeosaurus* belongs to a lineage of saurischian colossi known as sauropods, which include the largest land vertebrates of all time, some reaching a mass of over eighty tons. However, *Dicraeosaurus* is fortunate: Nature has furnished him with merely a half-dozen or so tons to locomote and sustain. He, like all his sauropod brethren, is a herbivore. *Dicraeosaurus* is distinctive for his moderately short (for a sauropod), high-spined neck, extremely long tail, and for the forking of the vertebral spines back to the hips.

Brachyphyllum

Nilssonia

Sphenopteris

Dictyozamites

Zamites

In several sauropods (including *Dicraeosaurus*) the position of the nasal openings above the eyes and the general skull architecture has led Dr. Walter P. Coombs, Jr. (Amherst College) to suggest that some sauropods possibly had well-developed snouts, perhaps even a proboscis similar to those of elephants and tapirs.*

For decades scientists generally believed that sauropods spent most of their existence in water, because it seemed impossible for even their pillar-like limbs to support such tremendous bulk on dry land for any considerable lengths of time. Recent studies of sauropod environments and limb-structure, however, now argue against an aquatic existence for these dinosaurs. In the North American Morrison Formation, for instance, where sauropod bones are especially abundant, there is little evidence of lakes deep enough to support giant sauropod bodies.

The earliest known sauropods (*Sauropodopus, Deuterosauropodopus*) left only their footprints on ancient South African deltas, near the dawn of late Triassic times, about two hundred million years ago. The most ancient actual sauropod bones (*Barapasaurus*) were deposited in Indian river sediments (Kota Formation) approximately 180 million years ago.

(Only wood *(Dadoxylon)* is known from Tendaguru; we have therefore relied on contemporary plants from other African areas (especially South Africa and Morocco) for our two Tendaguru scenes.)

*It must be stressed that we will probably never have direct evidence for sauropod trunks, but it is an interesting suggestion, and we wanted to take this opportunity to see just what a sauropod would look like with a trunk!

At Kindope, a site a few miles north of Tendaguru, a pit fifty to sixty feet deep was dug, covering an area of approximately three thousand square feet. Bone after bone of the stegosaur *Kentrosaurus* was extracted until an astounding wealth of material, representing over fifty individuals, was collected.

Sixteen-foot-long *Kentrosaurus* has plates and spikes arranged along the neck, back, and tail. The plates are restricted to the neck and front of the back; posterior to this are eight pairs of sharp spines, some more than two feet long. Two specialized spikes with expanded bases jut out from the back of the hips. *Kentrosaurus* is perhaps most closely related to the earlier European stegosaur, *Lexovisaurus*, but the armor of the latter is more varied.

The zenith of stegosaur development is reached during the Late Jurassic Period, though some supposed Cretaceous stegosaurs have been described. Of these, the only undoubted stegosaur is *Wuerhosaurus*, recently described from the Early Cretaceous Tugulo Series of Sinkiang, northwestern China.

Attenuate, nineteen-foot *Elaphrosaurus* is commonly placed in the theropod family Coeluridae, although it may actually belong in a family of its own. Possible elaphrosaurs, some of very large size, are also known from the Egyptian Late Cretaceous.

Nilssonia

Kentrosaurus

Zamites   *Cladophlebis*

Brachyphyllum

Elaphrosaurus

Taeniopteris

Dictyozamites

Zamites

Cladophlebis

g Irons '75

Pterophyllum

Sequoia

Cladophlebis

Yabeinosaurus

Czekanowskia

Shantangosuchus

Mesoclupea

On the eve of the Late Jurassic
Period 155 million years ago, an arm of
the Arctic Ocean moves southward across
Russia to connect with the Tethys Sea, leaving
Asia isolated from the rest of Laurasia. While much
of Europe is on the bottom of fluctuating seas, Asia is, in
contrast, an enormous emergent land with a vast system of lakes and
rivers. This is the home of the sanke-necked mamenchisaurs.

Sauropods with twenty-foot necks have been familiar to scientists and lay-
men alike for decades, but the recent discovery of *Mamenchisaurus* in Szechuan,
China, with fully thirty-three feet of throat dazzles even the most jaded scientist.

Mamenchisaurus, with its nineteen, elongated neck vertebrae, so impressed its
describer, Dr. C. C. Young (the leading authority on Chinese Mesozoic vertebrates), he
put the creature in its own family, the Mamenchisauridae. The entire skeleton, now mounted
at Peking, is over sixty-two feet in length, but the end of the tail is missing. If the tail assumes
the long, whiplash termination of many other sauropods, *Mamenchisaurus* may have reached the
seventy-five or eighty foot mark.

Barosaurus, a member of the closely related Diplodocidae, present in North America and East Africa, possibly exceeded ninety feet, and the neck of an undescribed barosaur in the American Museum of Natural History
in New York may have approached the length of that of *Mamenchisaurus*. Dr. James Jensen (Brigham Young University)
recently discovered a remarkably large sauropod which he affectionately refers to as "*Supersaurus*," because the specimen as
yet has no scientific name. The "supersaur" (perhaps related to the immense, long-armed *Brachiosaurus*) may well be the largest dinosaur of all time, and a single neck vertebra is reported to be five feet long! Visions of a 50-foot neck come to mind!

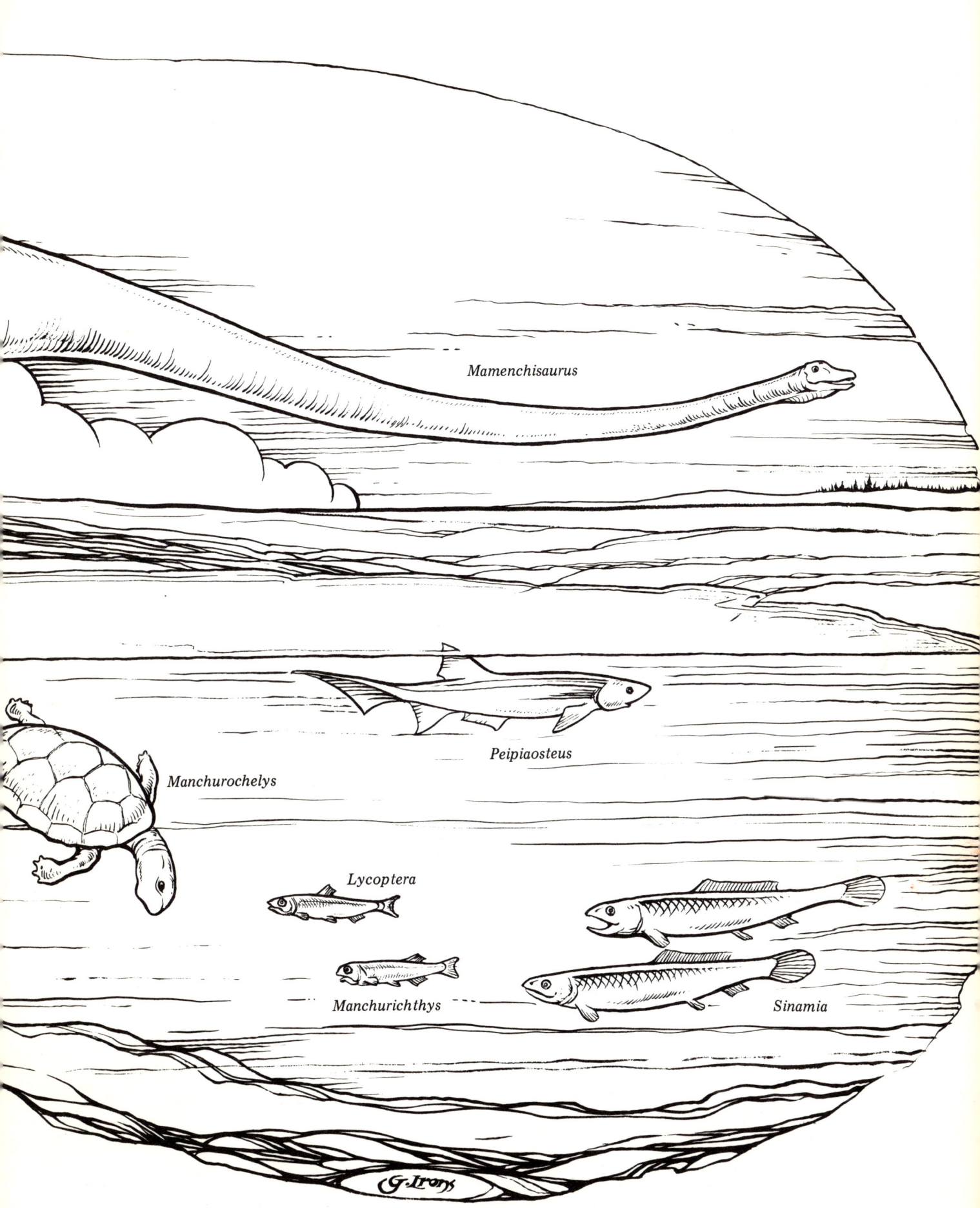

Mamenchisaurus

Peipiaosteus

Manchurochelys

Lycoptera

Manchurichthys

Sinamia

(The flora in our illustration is based on Late Jurassic specimens from Manchuria and Japan. It is interesting to note that the redwood *(Sequoia)* first appears in Late Jurassic beds of Manchuria, as well as North America (Morrison Formation).

Near the closing phases of the Jurassic, one hundred and forty-five million years ago, two large islands, one where the Black Forest now exists, the other near Regensburg, some two hundred and fifty miles to the east, are the major land areas present in southern Germany. Coral reefs separate these emergent regions from the open seas, and shallow lagoons are created between the reefs and land. Countless varieties of animals (including *Gnathosaurus* and *Anurognathus*) are buried and preserved in fine lime mud on these lagoonal floors.

Gnathosaurus is one of the largest Late Jurassic pterosaurs. Its eleven-inch skull is provided with numerous, elongated, needle-like teeth, and a high bony comb tops the snout. The gnathosaurs belong to the Ctenochasmatidae, a family of plankton-eating pterodactyloids. The little anurognathids, found in Russia (*Batrachognathus*) as well as southern Germany (*Anurognathus*), are rhamphorhynchoids, although their short tails distinguish them from other members of the suborder.

The most controversial of the German island dwellers are the remarkable dinosaur-birds (*Archaeopteryx*). Until the last half decade, three skeletons of this much celebrated "first bird" were known. In the 1970's, two more specimens were "discovered." One of these, an incomplete skeleton, was actually found over a century ago, but, because it was mis-identified as just another pterosaur, it lay unappreciated in a Dutch museum drawer for generations. Professor John H. Ostrom recently exposed the true identity of this long neglected specimen.

Much more important is a beautiful skeleton of a young *Archaeopteryx* collected near Eichstatt (Bavaria) in 1973. This fossil demonstrates beyond any reasonable doubt that *Archaeopteryx* is much more dinosaur-like than bird-like. Ostrom believes *Archaeopteryx* was a ground-living, theropod descendent which used its feathered forelimbs to snare or knock down prey (insects and other small creatures) rather than for flight.

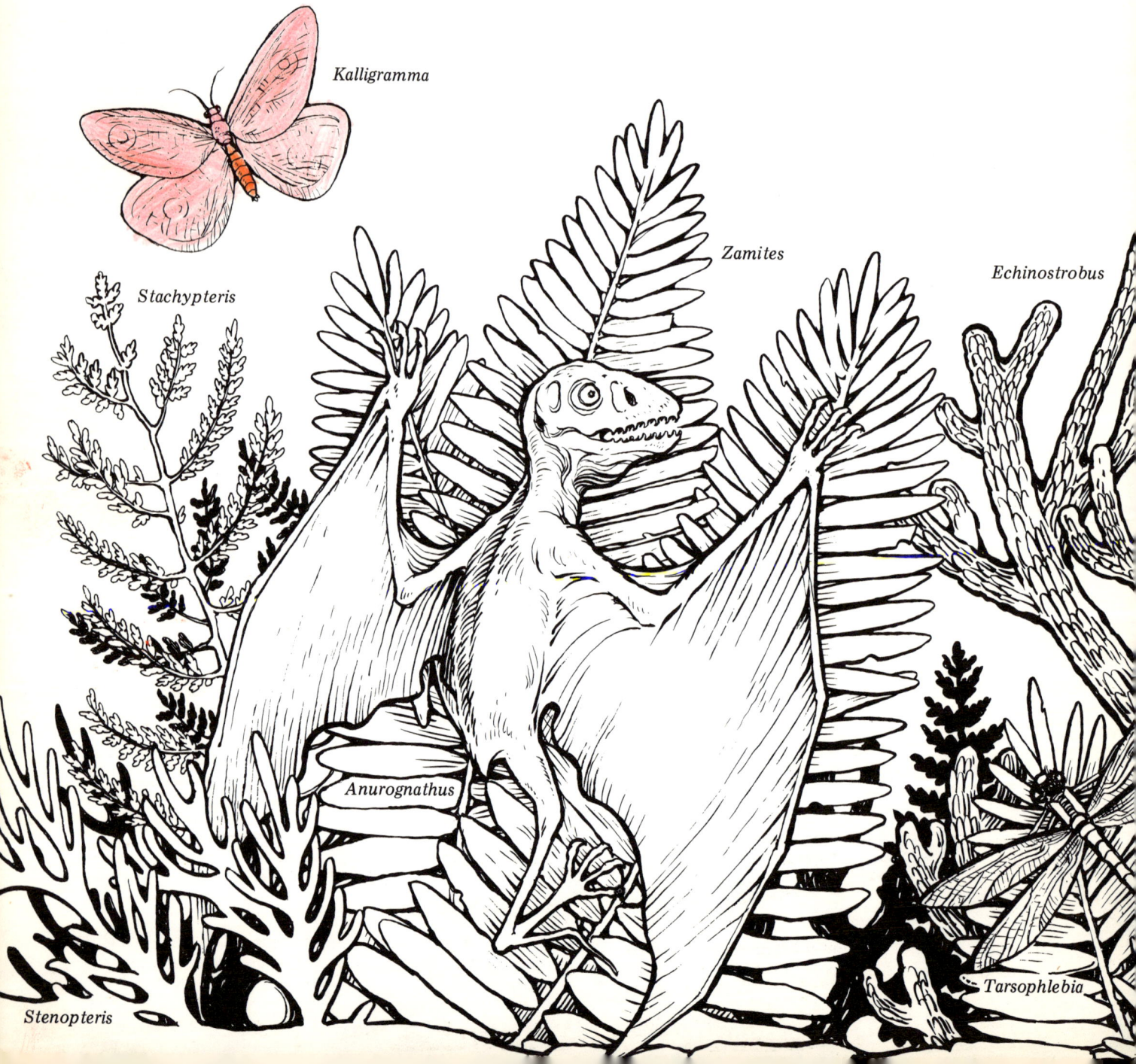

Kalligramma

Zamites

Echinostrobus

Stachypteris

Anurognathus

Tarsophlebia

Stenopteris

(The plants illustrated are based on contemporary German and French specimens.)

Furcifolium

Gnathosaurus

Cyrtophylites

Scleropteris

Swamps, lakes, and rivers embellish Wyoming and Montana during Cloverly times (the Early Cretaceous Period), one hundred and five million years ago. An arm of the Arctic Ocean is transgressing towards this region, as is a shallow epicontinental sea from the Gulf of Mexico. However, these waters will not flood Wyoming and Montana for several million years to come.

Death stalks the Cloverly in incomparable splendor —*Deinonychus*. Pound for pound it is the most ferocious demon of the dinosaur world. *Deinonychus* is the earliest of a line of especially hellish theropods, the dromaeosaurs. These diminutive brutes, mostly under a dozen feet long, possess the usual theropod implements of slaughter (i.e. a mouth full of sharp teeth and wicked, clawed hands), but something new is added to this deadly inventory. The second toe of the hind foot carries a huge, scimitar-like claw, always held well off the ground. Its purpose is grotesquely simple and to the point, ripping open a victim's belly in a single swipe!

Only petrified logs and fungus specimens have been collected. Investigations suggest that the region is usually very rainy, with heavy foliage.

Tempskya

Deinonychus

Plants illustrated in our scene are based on nearby Canadian records.

Sapindopsis

Fontaine

Acrostichopteris

Sagenopteris

Liriodendropsis

Magnolia

With the dawn of late Cretaceous times, ninety-five million years ago, an arm of the Tethys Sea pushes southward over North Africa. On the fringes of this gradual transgression, coastal swamps are produced which in time will be covered by the newly formed sea. It is difficult to imagine that the Sahara Desert of modern times was then a region of lagoons and estuaries, and supported a lush vegetation of magnolias, camphor trees, and laurels, as well as ferns and cycads. The climate was warm and dry, but certainly not as arid as it is now. Early snakes and perhaps the most ancient of snapping turtles are among its more inconspicuous denizens. Dinosaur and crocodile titans, in contrast, cast a horrific spell over this world.

Prior to the Late Cretaceous, nature had introduced huge-clawed theropods, crested-theropods, horned theropods, and perhaps even feathered theropods; now Egyptian swamps behold another theropod fad, sail-backed *Spinosaurus*. Why are the spines of the vertebrae lengthened to as much as two yards in *Spinosaurus*? We have no idea. Other long-spined theropods exist elsewhere, but they don't appear to be closely related to the fifty-foot giant, sole member of the family Spinosauridae.

A huge, six-foot long crocodile skull *(Stomatosuchus)* was collected with the spinosaur skeleton in the Baharije Oasis, over sixty years ago. For thirty years this material was housed in Munich, Germany, until it was destroyed by a bomb during World War II.

Spinosaurus

Cinnamomum
(camphor tree)

Frenelopsis

Nelumbites

Stomatosuchus

The Mongolian climate ranges from semi-arid to temperate ninety million years ago, but even in dry regions lush vegetation flourishes around the many lakes present. Flowering plants (angiosperms) become the predominant vegetation at this time in Asia and everywhere else (largely replacing conifers, ginkgos, cycadophytes and ferns so common in earlier Mesozoic times), and we may imagine the lake shores of Mongolia graced with willow, poplar, oak, sycamore and camphor trees, plus an undergrowth of holly, buckthorn, hercules club, spicebush and viburnum.[1] Like Caesar suddenly cast into modern Manhattan, the dinosaur finds himself in a world of strange, new trees (the same kinds that will support tree-houses for the children of 20th Century man).

Fifteen to twenty-foot *Bactrosaurus*, living in or near Mongolian lakes, is one of the earliest members of a family of armorless ornithischians, the Hadrosauridae, or duck-billed dinosaurs. Later Hadrosaurs often developed bizarre head-crests, and one hadrosaur recently discovered in Baja California, must have weighed over twenty tons in life, making it the most majestic of all known Ornithischia.[2]

The forelimbs of the huge Mongolian theropod, *Chilantaisaurus*, are enormous and well-adapted with great, hooked claws for tearing the life from its victims, the bactrosaurs.

[1] Though practically no plant fossils have been reported from Mongolian sediments of this age, other Asiatic regions have yielded excellent fossils which enable us to form a fairly good picture of ancient Mongolian plant life in watered areas.

[2] The hadrosaurs will be described in detail in the forthcoming Bellerophon book, *The Last of the Dinosaurs*.

Ilex
(holly)

Viburnum

Bactrosaurus

Platanus
(sycamore)

Platanus
(sycamore)

Chilantaisaurus

Viburnum

Ilex
(holly)

G. Irons

The chilantaisaurs are dead, two million decades pass, Mongolia changes. The former semi-arid climate intensifies to one of uncompromising aridity. The sharp edge of hot, dry winds, armed with particles of sand, slash relentlessly. Sand dunes radiate in every direction, seemingly forever, and mortiferous beds of quicksand offer the only permanent relief from the wicked elements in these the Djadochta times. Lakes and ponds are present here and there, enabling communities of tiny mammals, lizards, strange diminutive crocodiles, and various dinosaurs to survive this savage place.

Large meat-eating theropods are rare in the Djadochta; instead, a series of small, highly rapacious theropods are the principal killers. *Oviraptor*, perhaps eight or ten feet long, is toothless, but probably powerfully beaked, which more than makes up for its lack of dental equipment. It is usually classified with the "ostrich-dinosaurs" (Ornithomimidae), but the short, lightly built skull is so peculiar, we have little doubt *Oviraptor* is only distantly related to the ornithomimids. The hands of *Oviraptor* are relatively enormous, with extremely elongated, slender fingers—excellent for grasping prey such as the Djadochta monitor, *Telmasaurus*, seen in our illustration.

Oviraptor literally means "egg-stealer" because the specimen was discovered within inches of a nest of dinosaur eggs. It is believed that *Oviraptor* might have been attempting to steal the eggs when it died.

Saurornithoides is related to the dromaeosaurs and, like them, exhibits an enlarged belly-slashing claw on the hind foot. However, the bones enclosing the brain of *Saurornithoides* are specialized beyond those of dromaeosaurs; this character, plus others, have led scientists to place it in a family of its own, the Saurornithoididae. Late Cretaceous *Stenonychosaurus* from North America is a close relative.

Saurornithoides

Telmasaurus

Oviraptor

Vrons·75

Alzadasaurus

Clidastes

Scapanorhyncus

Calcichelys

Enchodus

Sauranodon

Triaenaspis

Archelon

Isurus

Tylosaurus

75 million years ago, western Kansas is covered by the Niobrara Sea. This sea is part of a watery corridor extending from the Gulf of Mexico to Canada—thus dividing what will be the future United States into western and eastern halves. COME SPEND TWO GLORIOUS WEEKS AT THE SHORE OF THE BEAUTIFUL NIOBRARA SEA; PLENTY OF TIME FOR QUIET, RELAXING SWIMS IN THE CALM, WARM, SHALLOW WATERS. Sounds very nice! But alas, these magnificent waters are infested with twenty-five-foot sharks, terrible-toothed fishes, dozen-foot, sharp-beaked turtles, a multitude of huge, paddled, marine lizards (mosasaurs), plus a varied assortment of other nightmare creatures.

Mosasaurs are known only from Late Cretaceous rocks, but were cosmopolitan in their distribution and must have been present in astounding numbers. They are closely related to the monitor lizards of today's tropics. Ram-nosed *Tylosaurus*, one of the largest of Kansas mosasaurs, reached lengths up to forty feet (*Hainosaurus*, a close relative from Belgium, is estimated to have a length of 56 feet—the all-time record for lizards). Another Kansas mosasaur, *Clidastes*, averaged a length of merely ten feet.

The ichthyosaurs, common in earlier times, are extinct by now, but the plesiosaurs continue to flourish. Thirty-foot *Alzadasaurus* belongs to a family of especially long-necked plesiosaurs, the Elasmosauridae.

Taxodium

Onoclea

Trons '74

Panoplosaurus

Seventy-two million years ago, most of Texas is under shallow seas; in southwestern Texas, swamps bordering these seas are home for a particularly impressive and dreadful killer. On a swamp bank, almost hidden by lush vegetation, this monster appears only as a dark, gleaming formless terror of astounding size; here it lies motionless, but alert and waiting. It is not a dinosaur, as one might expect because of its bulk, but the all-time colossus of the crocodile world—*Phobosuchus*.

Until recently, *Phobosuchus* was known only from a few broken bones and some thick armor plates (scutes) collected from the Aguja Formation of Big Bend National Park, Texas, and the Judith River Formation of Montana. This material was important in establishing the presence in North America of a gigantic, Late Cretaceous crocodile, possibly more than 50' long, but it gave us little other data. But a huge, well-preserved

Phobosuchus

skull of *Phobosuchus* has recently been discovered in the Big Bend region by Dr. Wann Langston, (University of Texas, Austin), which will clear up many questions concerning this monster.

Even more curious than the immense phobosuchians is the fifteen-foot ankylosaur, *Panoplosaurus*, resembling an armadillo a thousand times magnified. The Ankylosauria, a suborder of heavily armored, wide-bodied ornithischians, with broad, low heads and massive lower jaws, are only recorded from Cretaceous rocks.* Their short heavy limbs terminate in stubby, hooved feet. The armor, consisting of rows of keeled plates, is developed over the neck, back, and tail.

Recent investigations by Dr. Walter P. Coombs, Jr., demonstrate there are two ankylosaur families—the Nodosauridae and the Ankylosauridae. The former, including *Panoplosaurus*, are characterized by pear-shaped heads (when viewed from above), large spikes on the sides (especially large in the shoulder region), solid armor plates, and a clubless tail. The Ankylosauridae have triangular heads, small or absent lateral spikes, armor plates hollowed out underneath, and a tail terminating in a very large bony club—great for breaking theropod shins.

Panoplosaurus occurs in Montana, Alberta (Canada), and perhaps South Dakota, as well as in the Aguja sediments of Texas. Thanks to Dr. Walter Combs, Jr., Pratt Museum, Amherst College, for giving us unpublished data on ankylosaurian dinosaurs. (Because no plant fossils have ever been collected from the Aguja Formation, we have used specimens from the roughly contemporary Vermejo Formation of New Mexico and Colorado, and the Kirtland Formation of New Mexico.)

* Some scientists consider the Early Jurassic *Scelidosaurus* a primitive ankylosaur, but the evidence has not been convincing.

Prenocephale

Sabalites

Osmunda

Numerous meandering streams flow across Mongolia, seventy-two million years ago. The great sand dunes of early Dja-dochta times are replaced with fertile plains, and the climate now alternates with seasonal rains and dry periods. The deposition of the Nemegt Formation is taking place.

The Nemegt ornithischians *Homalocephale* and *Prenocephale* are dome-head dinosaurs (suborder Pachycephalosauria). The researches of Mr. L. Sprague de Camp and Dr. Peter M. Galton conclude that these animals use their thick-boned skulls as battering rams, just as mountain sheep use their horns today. The pachycephalosaurs are usually no larger than big dogs, but they are stocky and slow-moving. The front limbs are tiny, so there can be little doubt these animals are bipedal. The hips are very wide, and the extremely thick and heavy tail is important as a counter-balance to the large head.

The solid-bone dome is especially high in *Prenocephale*. Its front teeth are long and sharp, while those at the back of the jaws are blunt. Despite these knife-like front teeth, *Prenocephale* lives exclusively on vegetation. In *Homalocephale* the dome is only slightly developed. Though the Mongolian pachycephalosaurs are small, a later form from North America (*Pachyce-phalosaurus*) probably out-weighs a full-grown grizzly bear.

We are indebted for our knowledge of Nemegt life to Polish, Russian, and Mongolian scientists, who have conducted a series of expeditions to the Nemegt Basin.

Homalocephale

Mongolemys

Nyssa
(tupelo gum)

Gallimimus

Far outnumbering the pachycephalosaurs in the Nemegt are two types of theropods, radically different from each other—*Gallimimus* and *Tarbosaurus*.

Thirty-foot *Gallimimus* is the largest representative of the Ornithomimidae, the "ostrich dinosaurs". Though small-headed and toothless, the gallimimids are quick, probably among the swiftest of dinosaurs, and when provoked can give a deadly kick with their large, sharp-clawed hind feet. The bulky, huge-headed tarbosaurs belong to the horrific Tyrannosauridae, a family of gigantic devastators stalking North America and East Asia during latest Cretaceous times. The tyrannosaurid skull is especially enormous and massive. The vertebrae are short and high, so the neck and trunk are shorter and thicker than in most theropods. The front limbs are reduced to ridiculously tiny proportions and end in only two digits.

Forty-foot *Tarbosaurus* is the only known determinate Asian tyrannosaur, though fragmentary remains probably belonging to other tyrannosaurid genera do occur in several Asian formations. At least three genera of tyrannosaurs (*Albertosaurus*, *Daspletosaurus*, and *Tyrannosaurus*) are present in North America.

The dinosaur graveyard in the Nemegt Basin is haunted by even mightier horrors than the tarbosaur. The theropod *Deinocheirus* is known only from front limbs of colossal size. Its claws alone are each a foot long, and in life they were covered with a horny sheath which increased this measurement considerably. The great hands of *Deinocheirus* show similarities to those of the ornithomimids, though it obviously belongs to a family of its own (Deinocheiridae). *Therezinosaurus*, perhaps also a deinocheirid, is merely known from claws, but these are almost a yard in length!

(No plants have been described from the Nemegt Formation, so we have relied on contemporary plant fossils from other Asian regions (especially Japan) for our Nemegt illustrations.)

Pinus

Nilssonia

Tarbosaurus

Anemia

Frons '75

Sixty-four million years ago, the Mesozoic Era is nearing completion, and the great dinosaurs will soon disappear forever. However, as if all of Nature's forces combined to demonstrate for one last time an ability for devilish invention, a supreme monster is ushered forth, this time equipped with wings over fifty feet across.

By far the largest of all flying creatures, *Quetzalcoatlus* was only recently discovered in the Late Cretaceous Tornillo Formation of the Big Bend region of southern Texas. It is undoubtedly a pterosaur, and the slender, ten-foot neck and toothless lower jaw are features similar to those of certain members of the suborder Pterodactyloidea. *Quetzalcoatlus* probably lived a vulturous existence in the hilly upland regions, seeking out dinosaur carcasses as its principal food source. Douglas A. Lawson, a graduate student at Berkeley, discovered the "quetzal" (Lawson's pet name for the Texas giant), and he is currently investigating the creature.

Alamosaurus is the last of the sauropod dinosaurs. It occurs not only in Texas, but also in New Mexico, Utah, and perhaps in Wyoming.

Alamosaurus

Asplenium

Nelumbo

Quetzalcoatlus
- the Giant Pterosaur
(Wing tip to tip: 50+ feet!)

Fraxinus

Cercidiphyllum

Vitis

Asplenium

No plant fossils have been discovered in the dinosaur-bearing portion of the Tornillo Formation. We have used contemporary plants from North American sites.

Sixty-four million years ago, the Scollard Member of the Paskapoo Formation is undergoing deposition in central Alberta. Mountain ranges are slowly rising just to the west, and the seas, so near a few million years earlier, have regressed hundreds of miles to the southeast. Detritus, washed down these new ranges by streams and rivers, has accumulated to form plains where the dinosaurs of the Scollard now roam.

The swamp and lake-dwelling hadrosaurs are nearly absent in these upland plains. The ceratopsians, a suborder of large-headed, often horn-faced ornithischians, thrive here. The giant of the group, *Triceratops*, reaching a length of perhaps thirty feet and probably weighing upwards of a dozen tons, is an abundant Scollard form. *Leptoceratops*, in contrast to this huge relative, is a mere two yards long, hornless, and lacks the head frill displayed in *Triceratops*.

In *Leptoceratops* and its allies (family Protoceratopsidae), the fore limbs are considerably shorter than the hind, all the limb bones are long and slender, and the toes are clawed rather than hooved. These features, plus those of the skull already mentioned, easily separate the little protoceratopsids from *Triceratops* and its allies (Ceratopsidae*). A new protoceratopsid (*Bagaceratops*) has just recently been discovered in Mongolia (Barun Goyot Formation) by Polish paleontologists.

Palaeosaniwa, a giant monitor lizard, is a close relative of the modern Komodo dragon-lizard of the East Indies. Its fossils have not yet been found in Scollard sediments, but do come from the contemporary Lance Formation of eastern Wyoming, and earlier beds (Oldman Member of the Judith River Formation) of central Alberta. It therefore possibly stalked central Alberta during Scollard times, though it may have preferred wet, lowland areas.

*The ceratopsids will be discussed in detail in our forthcoming book, *The Last of the Dinosaurs*.

Note: The supernova theory discussed on the opposite page must, like its predecessors, be regarded with skepticism, but it is imaginative and highly novel.

Sequoia

Palaeosaniwa

(Plants based on Scollard specimens.)

VIOLIN I

DUET

in A major, K.331
for Two Violins *

VIOLIN I

WOLFGANG AMADEUS MOZART
(1756-1791)

DUET

in A major, K.331

for Two Violins *

VIOLIN I

WOLFGANG AMADEUS MOZART
(1756-1791)

VAR. 3.

VIOLIN I

VAR. 4.
Allegro.

VIOLIN I